MUSCLES AND MOVEMENT

Izzi Howell

WAYLAND
www.waylandbooks.co.uk

First published in Great Britain in 2017 by Wayland
ISBN: 978 1 5263 0680 7
10 9 8 7 6 5 4 3 2 1

Wayland
An imprint of Hachette Children's Group
Part of Hodder & Stoughton
Carmelite House
50 Victoria Embankment
London EC4Y 0DZ

An Hachette UK Company
www.hachette.co.uk
www.hachettechildrens.co.uk

A catalogue for this title is available from
the British Library
Printed and bound in China

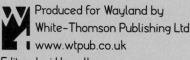

Produced for Wayland by
White-Thomson Publishing Ltd
www.wtpub.co.uk
Editor: Izzi Howell
Design: Clare Nicholas

Picture credits:
Getty: GlobalStock *title page* and 15, luamduan 5bl, Delpixart 8tl, GlobalP 9t, USO 11c, FatCamera 12, mauribo 13, spxChrome 14t, Freder 14bl, zefart 18–19b, OceanBodhi 20; Shutterstock: Arlene Gapusan *cover* t, Valentyna Chukhlyebova *cover* b, Potapov Alexander 4l, Aila Images 4r, Potapov Alexander 5t, Suphatthra China 5br, Skalapendra 6, holbox 7t, xpixel 7c, hsagencia 7b, ninii 8tr, Marco Tomasini 8b, Eric Isselee 9bl and 17c, givaga 9br, javarman 10l, VaLiza 10r, BORINA OLGA 11t, RusticBoy 11b, Johan Swanepoel 13, Svetlana Foote 13, pirita 13, ArtFamily 13, Richard Peterson 13, Vladimir Melnik 14br, EpicStockMedia 16, Rich Carey 17t, Vangert 17b, Kirsanov Valeriy Vladimirovich 18t, Nejron Photo 19tl, Ambient Ideas 19tr, RamonaS 21t, RamonaS 21b.

Should there be any inadvertent omission, please apply to the publisher for rectification.

The author, Izzi Howell, is a writer and editor specialising in children's educational publishing.

Contents

Skeleton

Inside a human body, there is a skeleton made of bones joined together.

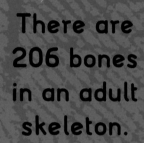

There are 206 bones in an adult skeleton.

Our skeleton helps us to move. It also protects the insides of our body.

protect: to keep safe

Some animals also
have a skeleton.

Squawk!

an ostrich

a gorilla

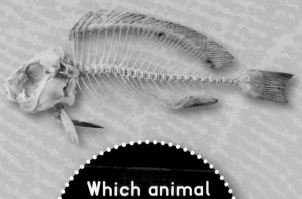

Which animal
does this
skeleton come
from?

Muscles

Humans and most animals have muscles inside their body. Muscles pull on our bones to help us move.

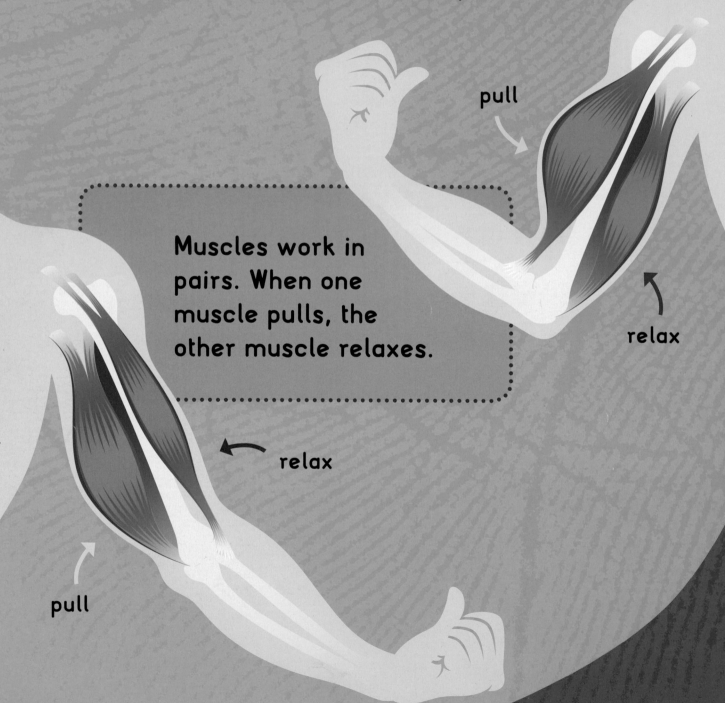

pull

relax

Muscles work in pairs. When one muscle pulls, the other muscle relaxes.

relax

pull

Some animals don't have skeletons, but they do have muscles. They use their muscles to move their body.

a jellyfish

a snail

an earthworm

Exoskeletons

Animals without a skeleton protect their body in other ways. Some animals have a hard covering on the outside of their body called an exoskeleton.

a ladybird

a crab

a clam

Which animal on page 7 has an exoskeleton?

Some animals need a bigger exoskeleton as they grow larger.

The praying mantis sheds its smaller exoskeleton. Then, it grows a bigger exoskeleton.

old exoskeleton

The hermit crab uses a shell from another animal as its exoskeleton. It finds a new, larger shell when it gets bigger.

Walking

Humans and some animals walk on two legs. One foot stays on the ground while the other foot lifts up and moves forwards.

a human

a penguin

Wait for me!

Many animals walk on four or more legs.

a dog

four legs

a Komodo dragon

four legs

six legs

an ant

Which animal moves on eight legs?

11

Running

Running is faster than walking. When we run, we bend our knees and push harder against the ground with our feet.

Sometimes, both our feet come off the ground.

Some animals can run much faster than humans.

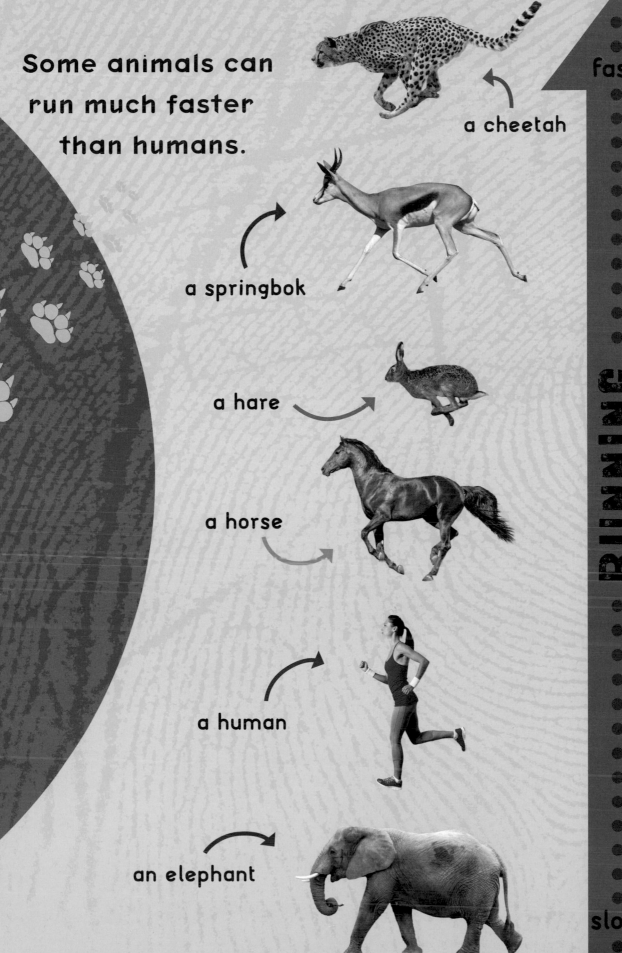

a cheetah

a springbok

a hare

a horse

a human

an elephant

RUNNING

fast

slow

Jumping

To jump, humans and animals bend their knees. Then, they push themselves up off the ground.

Humans and animals jump for many reasons.

a kangaroo

to get from one place to another

to move around

a polar bear

for fun!

a human

Swimming

Some animals that live in water swim to move around. Humans can also learn to swim.

Animals use different parts of their body to swim.

a sea turtle

front flippers

a frog

back legs

Which body parts do humans use to swim?

a goldfish

whole body and tail

Flying

Some animals can fly.
Flying animals have wings.

Screech!

a bat

Animals fly by flapping their
wings up and down. This pushes
them through the air.

a parrot

a butterfly

a seagull

19

Special movement

Some animals move in special ways.

An octopus sucks in water and then shoots it out of its body to push itself forwards.

Snakes do not have any arms or legs. They use their muscles to move their body from side to side. This pushes them forwards.

Mudskippers are fish that can live on land or in water. In water, they use their fins to swim. On land, they walk on their fins.

Gasp!

Human and animal movement

Mammals

bat
cheetah
dog
elephant
gorilla
hare
horse
human
kangaroo
polar bear
springbok

FEATURES

skeleton, usually move on four legs, but not always

Birds

ostrich
parrot
penguin
seagull

FEATURES

skeleton, walk on two legs

Fish

goldfish
mudskipper

FEATURES

skeleton, swim

Amphibians

frog

FEATURES

skeleton, usually move on four legs

Minibeasts

ant
butterfly
earthworm
ladybird
praying mantis
snail

FEATURES

no skeleton, sometimes have an exoskeleton

Invertebrates

clam
crab
hermit crab
jellyfish
octopus

FEATURES

no skeleton, sometimes have an exoskeleton

Reptiles

Komodo dragon
sea turtle
snake

FEATURES

skeleton, usually move on four legs, but not always

Index

Answers

p5 — A fish
p8 — A snail
p11 — A spider
p17 — Arms and legs

HUMAN BODY ANIMAL BODIES

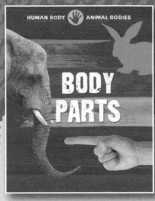

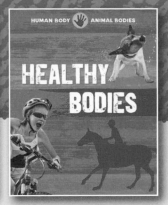

978 1 5263 0676 0

978 1 5263 0678 4

978 1 5263 0680 7

978 1 5263 0682 1

BODY PARTS
Human and animal bodies
Head
Neck
Skin
Hair and fur
Arms, wings and fins
Hands
Legs
Feet
Human and animal classification

HEALTHY BODIES
Healthy bodies
Diet
Animal diets
Water
Sleeping
Exercise
Keeping warm
Keeping clean
Feeling ill
Human and animal classification

MUSCLES AND MOVEMENT
Skeleton
Muscles
Exoskeletons
Walking
Running
Jumping
Swimming
Flying
Special movement
Human and animal movement

SENSES
What are senses?
Sight
Looking around
Hearing
Taste
Different tastes
Touch
Smell
Special senses
Human and animal senses

WAYLAND
www.waylandbooks.co.uk